Journey of the
DRAGONFLIES

BY ANNERENEÈ GOYETTE

Gareth Stevens
PUBLISHING

Please visit our website, www.garethstevens.com. For a free color catalog of all our high-quality books, call toll free 1-800-542-2595 or fax 1-877-542-2596.

Cataloging-in-Publication Data

Names: Goyette, AnneReneè.
Title: Journey of the dragonflies / AnneReneè Goyette.
Description: New York : Gareth Stevens Publishing, 2019. | Series: Massive animal migrations | Includes index.
Identifiers: ISBN 9781538216507 (pbk.) | ISBN 9781538216491 (library bound) | ISBN 9781538216514 (6 pack)
Subjects: LCSH: Dragonflies--Juvenile literature. | Dragonflies--Life cycles--Juvenile literature.
Classification: LCC QL520.G69 2019 | DDC 595.7'33--dc23

First Edition

Published in 2019 by
Gareth Stevens Publishing
111 East 14th Street, Suite 349
New York, NY 10003

Copyright © 2019 Gareth Stevens Publishing

Designer: Katelyn E. Reynolds
Editor: Joan Stoltman

Photo credits: Cover, p. 1 Alex Huizinga/NIS/Minden Pictures/Getty Images; cover, pp. 1–24 (background) Vadim Georgiev/Shutterstock.com; cover, pp. 1–24 (background) CS Stock/Shutterstock.com; p. 5 boyphare/Shutterstock.com; p. 7 Brown Bear/Windmill Books/UIG via Getty Images; p. 9 (inset) enciktat/Shutterstock.com; p. 9 (main) Ondrej Prosicky/Shutterstock.com; p. 11 © iStockphoto.com/geoffsp; p. 13 © iStockphoto.com/jorgriommi; p. 15 Paul Reeves Photography/Shutterstock.com; p. 17 (map) Serban Bogdan/Shutterstock.com; p. 17 (inset) Shyamal/Wikipedia.org; p. 19 Hans Christiansson/Shutterstock.com; p. 21 (kids) MANDY GODBEHEAR/Shutterstock.com; p. 21 (paper and pencil) Be Good/Shutterstock.com.

Printed in the United States of America

CPSIA compliance information: Batch #CS18GS: For further information contact Gareth Stevens, New York, New York at 1-800-542-2595.

CONTENTS

WORDS IN THE GLOSSARY APPEAR IN **BOLD** TYPE
THE FIRST TIME THEY ARE USED IN THE TEXT.

Incredible INSECTS!

They can fly **backward**! They can hit speeds of 20 miles (32 km) per hour! They've been on Earth for 285 million years—before dinosaurs! They even eat pests like **mosquitoes** and flies!

The dragonfly is a colorful **insect** that lives near **freshwater** ponds, lakes, streams, and rivers. Dragonflies live everywhere except Antarctica! Some species, or kinds, never leave the place they were born. Other species **migrate**. Scientists recently discovered that some dragonfly species make the longest insect migration in the world!

> ## THERE'S MORE!
> SOME ANCIENT DRAGONFLIES HAD A 2.5-FOOT (0.76 M) **WINGSPAN** AND WERE LARGE ENOUGH TO EAT SMALL ANIMALS! THE DRAGONFLIES OF TODAY ARE MUCH SMALLER, THOUGH THEY LOOK ABOUT THE SAME!

Life CYCLE

Dragonflies start their life in freshwater as eggs. Migration is all about finding safe freshwater for the female dragonfly to lay her eggs. After **hatching,** dragonflies live underwater, sometimes for up to 6 years. They even breathe underwater!

Then they **molt** over and over, with a final molt in late spring or summer. Now they have bright colors and wings! Their wings need a few days to dry and harden. Some adult dragonflies only live a month, while others live up to a year.

THERE'S MORE!

DRAGONFLY YOUNG ARE CALLED NYMPHS! THEY PREFER WATER THAT DOESN'T MOVE MUCH AND DOESN'T HAVE A LOT OF FISH, LIKE STREAMS AND PONDS.

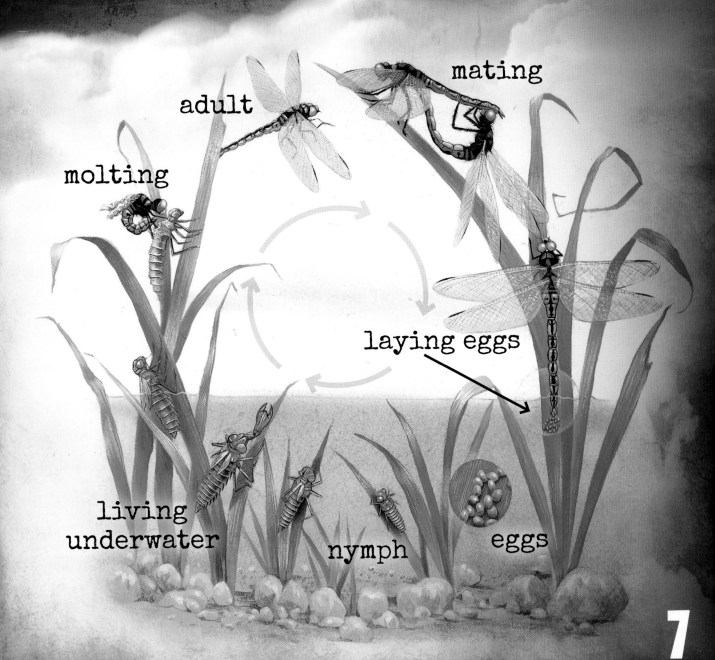

mating

adult

molting

laying eggs

living underwater

nymph

eggs

BEING EATEN!

Dragonflies are great hunters. Nymphs eat their weight in mosquito larvae several times a day! They also enjoy eating tadpoles, small fish, and other underwater insects.

Adults have two ways of hunting. Fliers fly around hunting for food. Perchers sit and watch for prey, then quickly fly after it once it gets close enough. Migrating species can be either kind of hunter. Both catch their food with their feet and crush it inside their mouth with their strong **jaws**! During migration, adult dragonflies stop every few days to hunt.

THERE'S MORE!

AVOIDING PREDATORS IS DIFFERENT IN THE WATER THAN IT IS IN THE AIR. NYMPHS PULL IN WATER AND THEN QUICKLY PUSH IT OUT TO GET AWAY. ADULTS CAN FLY FASTER THAN MOST PREDATORS!

Nymphs have to watch out for fish, frogs, toads, and other animals that live near water. Adults can get eaten by birds, spiders, frogs, fish, and even other dragonflies!

dragonfly eating a bug

9

Cool WINGS!

Flying takes a lot of **energy**. To last through a long migration, dragonflies have to use the energy they get from food carefully. Every time they beat their wings, energy is used.

But dragonflies have a trick! They have two sets of wings, which means they can **glide** really well and not beat their wings as often. In fact, dragonflies only have to beat their wings 30 times in 1 second. A bee, on the other hand, beats its wings 300 times in 1 second!

> **THERE'S MORE!**
>
> DRAGONFLIES CAN ALSO BEAT THEIR WINGS TOGETHER OR SEPARATELY, WHICH IS HOW THEY CAN FLY BACKWARD AND UP OR DOWN!

MIGRATION

Dragonflies migrate during the day, staying close to trees and plants. Scientists think they may have special cells in their body that tell them which direction they're headed!

Dragonflies probably know when it's time to move south in fall when there are several cold days in a row. They travel in a **swarm**, migrating south by riding cold winds that blow from north to south. In spring, they don't swarm for migration. Instead, they travel north by riding warm winds that blow from south to north.

> ### THERE'S MORE!
> THE DRAGONFLIES THAT FLY NORTH IN SPRING ARE THE CHILDREN OF THE DRAGONFLIES THAT HEADED SOUTH IN FALL!

Not every swarm of dragonflies is migrating. They sometimes gather in swarms to feed or mate.

13

The Green DARNER

The green darner is one of nine species of dragonfly that migrate a long way in North America. A few years ago, scientists glued a special tracking tool to the body of a few to track them during migration. As they flew, the scientists followed in an airplane.

Scientists had long wondered how dragonflies had the energy to fly long migrations. They discovered that the green darner stopped for 2 days to eat and rest every 3 days. This means dragonflies stop to get more energy throughout their migration!

> **THERE'S MORE!**
>
> SCIENTISTS ALSO DISCOVERED THAT GREEN DARNERS MIGRATE ALONG THE SAME PATHS AS BIRDS!

Scientists discovered that green darners can fly around 38 miles (61 km) a day. They saw one green darner fly 100 miles (160 km) in a day!

15

The Wandering GLIDER

A few years ago, scientists discovered that the longest insect migration in the world was flown by a tiny dragonfly called the wandering glider. These dragonflies fly 11,000 miles (18,000 km), or 400 million times their own body length! They're the only insects to migrate across an ocean!

Wandering gliders follow rain, eating insects in the air during flight. They stop every few days to eat and lay eggs in the pools made from heavy rains. Weeks later, those eggs hatch, and new dragonflies grow, molt, and continue on the journey!

> ### THERE'S MORE!
> WE DON'T KNOW HOW, BUT WANDERING GLIDERS ARE FOUND IN THE UNITED STATES, JAPAN, INDIA, AFRICA, AND SOUTH AMERICA. THE INSECTS ARE TOO SMALL, HOWEVER, TO GLUE TRACKING TOOLS ONTO!

Wandering gliders [...] the short rains of East Africa, then the summer rains of South Africa, then back to East Africa for long rains. Then they head back to India for the next monsoon season!

INDIA

AFRICA

Indian Ocean

wandering gliders

17

AND HOW?

The wandering glider migration is very dangerous. But by following rain all year long, they're able to find safe places to lay eggs everywhere they go. This means more wandering gliders are born than if the species stayed in one place and waited for rain.

Wandering gliders have very wide wings that are perfect for gliding long distances without flapping a lot. Their wings can also handle flying in strong winds, which means they can push farther forward during flight.

THERE'S MORE!

WANDERING GLIDERS FLY HIGHER THAN ANY OTHER DRAGONFLY SPECIES. THIS ALLOWS THEM TO RIDE WINDS THAT ARE HEADED IN THE DIRECTION THEY WANT TO GO ALL YEAR ROUND!

Many, many wandering gliders die during this huge migration, but it must be done.

19

Why Do Dragonflies MATTER?

Dragonflies are a very important part of the food chain. They eat many different kinds of insects. They're also an important food for birds, fish, and other animals. Scientists know that if dragonflies are dying in an area, something big is wrong!

We still know so little about dragonfly migration. A better understanding of insect swarms could help keep crops that people depend on alive. Discovering just how and where dragonflies migrate will help us learn about birds, weather, other insects, and so much more!

BECOME A CITIZEN SCIENTIST!

A group of scientists is studying dragonflies in North America. Let them know where dragonflies are showing up throughout the year by handing in your observations to migratorydragonflypartnership.org with an adult's help!

Write down species, date, and location for each sighting.

Dragonflies become more active once the day warms up.

Look out for dragonflies whenever you're near water!

It's easiest to tell what species a dragonfly is when it's sitting still on a plant!

If we don't know their migration paths and patterns, how can we help keep these dragonfly species safe?

You'll Need:

paper and pencil

21

GLOSSARY

backward: opposite to the usual way

energy: power used to do work

freshwater: water that is not salty

glide: to move in a smooth and graceful way

hatch: to break open or come out of

insect: a small, often winged, animal with six legs and three body parts

jaw: one of the body parts used for biting or chewing food

migrate: to move to warmer or colder places for a season, or to move from one area to another for feeding or having babies

molt: to shed, or get rid of, a hard outer covering that has become too small. Also, the act of shedding a hard outer covering that has become too small.

monsoon: the rainy season that occurs in southern Asia in the summer

mosquito: a small flying insect that bites the skin of people and animals and sucks their blood

swarm: a very large number of creatures moving together

vein: any one of the tubes that carry blood from parts of the body back to the heart

wingspan: the length between the tips of a pair of wings that are stretched out

FOR MORE INFORMATION

Books

Earley, Chris. *Dragonflies: Catching, Identifying, How and Where They Live.* Buffalo, NY: Firefly Books, 2013.

Ipcizade, Catherine. *Dazzling Dragonflies.* North Mankato, MN: Capstone Press, 2017.

Nelson, Robin. *Darting Dragonflies.* Minneapolis, MN: Lerner Publications, 2017.

Websites

14 Fun Facts About Dragonflies
smithsonianmag.com/science-nature/14-fun-facts-about-dragon-flies-96882693/
You'll be amazed reading just how cool dragonflies are!

Behavioral Videos
migratorydragonflypartnership.org/index/behavioralResources
Watch these amazing videos about how dragonflies act.

Field Guide to Migratory Dragonflies
migratorydragonflypartnership.org/uploads/_ROOT/File/MDP-field_guide.pdf
This printable guide will help you tell the difference between dragonflies while you're in field!

INDEX